T0299492

No Context Brits Presents

EVERYTHING IS GREAT

The Weird, Wild and Wonderful World of Modern Britain

For Rocco and Cali Rae

First published in Great Britain in 2024 by

Greenfinch
An imprint of Quercus Editions Limited
Carmelite House
50 Victoria Embankment
London EC4Y 0DZ

An Hachette UK company
The authorised representative in the EEA is Hachette Ireland, 8 Castlecourt Centre,
Castleknock Road, Castleknock, Dublin 15, D15 YF6A, Ireland

A CIP catalogue record for this book is available from the British Library

HB ISBN 978-1-52943-529-0
Ebook ISBN 978-1-52943-530-6

10 9 8 7 6 5 4 3 2 1

Interior design by James Pople
Cover design by Estuary English Ltd
Printed and bound in Great Britain by Clays Ltd, Elcograf S.p.A.

MIX
Paper | Supporting
responsible forestry
FSC
www.fsc.org   FSC® C104740

Papers used by Greenfinch are from well-managed forests and other responsible sources.

No Context Brits Presents

EVERYTHING IS GREAT

The Weird, Wild and Wonderful World of Modern Britain

Quercus

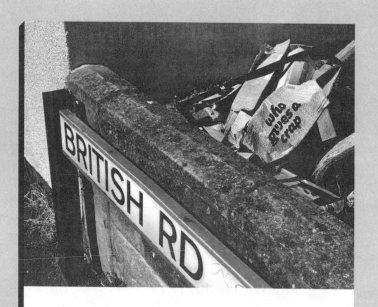

❝ Being British is about singing Karaoke in bars, eating Chinese noodles and Japanese sushi, drinking French wine, wearing Prada and Nike, dancing to Italian house music, listening to Cher, using an Apple Mac, holidaying in Florida and Ibiza and buying a house in Spain. ❞

Malcolm McLaren, the *Guardian*, January 1999.

CONTENTS

Hello!

Welcome to Britain. Great Britain, to be precise. And it is indeed great. No other country on Earth is named after just how great it is. Go check. There's no Great Canada, or Great Romania or Great Uruguay or United Greatness of America. No, *only* Great Britain is great enough to be named after just how great it is. So, yeah, we're even the greatest at nominative determinism. Take that, China!

Our 88,000-square-mile island empire is so special, in fact, that we don't need to get any better – not that we've been trying, to be fair. Why bother? We've got rolling green fields filled with pylons delivering fresh electricity to our front doors, ancient woodlands ideal for dogging and dumping old fridges, service stations as far as the eye can see, and millions of citizens who are quite happy being miserable. Hell, there's even a Greggs on every high street now. What more could we possibly want? In the face of so much global aggression and progression, Britain won't be bullied into budging for anyone. We're going nowhere. And that seems to suit us fine.

Modern Britain is a place where anything goes, where ordinary events become extraordinarily complicated for no reason whatsoever.

No Context Brits
@NoContextBrits

···

What do these taste like?

They probably taste of cigarettes and alcohol.

To celebrate Britain achieving this peak greatness, on April Fool's Day 2021, in the midst of a global lockdown, we gave life to **No Context Brits** on Twitter (now X). As the COVID-19 pandemic ravaged the globe, we suddenly had a lot of "spare time" to share with the citizens of Britain something that celebrated the current, topical peculiarities of these Sceptred Isles, but in a positive way. The account was meant to be a tongue-in-cheek parody of the land we love to whinge about as we came to the numbing revelation that this, the 2020s, is probably as good as Britain's going to get before the country ultimately enters its final spinning wheel of death phase.

. . . .

66 Brits are keen to stare and point (and laugh) at how funny their little Britain has become, like a car wreck on the motorway you slow down to check for mangled bodies. **99**

. . . .

That actually happened in 2022.

Brexit was the first domino to fall, then came our COVID-19 response, then "Partygate", then Liz Truss – you get the picture. If you dare remember, 2016–2023 was a tough time to be proud to be British. And yet, because of this crazy time (or despite it) the No Context Brits account continued to grow beyond our wildest horizons. Beyond even Hull.

Within a few months, the account blew up, proof, were it needed, that Brits are keen to stare and point (and laugh) at how little their Britain has become, like a car wreck on the motorway you slow down to check for mangled bodies. Only – we the people are the bodies. And Britain is the car wreck. Of course, fans of No Context Brits understood immediately that the memes we posted were not just laughing *at* Britain, they were laughing *with* Britain, because if there's one thing Britons understand above all else, it's that we do not take ourselves at all seriously. We kind of have the global monopoly on self-deprecation, after all. Just like we do delusions of grandeur. And Greggs.

This book is a celebration of all the things modern Britain loves about being British, and an insight into what it truly means to be Great and British at the same time in the 21st century, a time when the Mental Wellbeing Index just voted Britain as the second most miserable nation on Earth. (Uzbekistan took the crown, FYI. That's how bad it is.)

As affectionate as it is alarming, *Everything is Great* is a warts-and-all peek up Britain's blouse and takes a self-depreciating selfie at everything we can see, from our cuisine to our weather, our music to our collective refusal to scoop up our dogs' shit, and all the lairy bits in between we're usually too awkward to talk about.

So, welcome to Great Britain, come on in. Please wipe your feet.

• •

It was King James VI who first started calling Britain great when, in 1603, he named himself "King of Great Britain". The name stuck when the Acts of Union law passed in 1707, creating a united kingdom to be called "Great Britain".

• •

No Context Brits ✓
@NoContextBrits

Take that criminals.

Harsh but fair!

Made in Britain

Take a look around. Go on. Enjoy the view. Breathe it in. There's no doubt about it. Britain is the absolute best at being British. From Brown Willy (in Cornwall) to Twatt (in Orkney), and everywhere in between, no wet spot on the map has been missed by what we call "epic Britishness". You know, the type of stubborn Britishness you can't get out of your shirt no matter how hard you scrub to get that bastard clean.

Anyway, if you're looking for the best of Britain, stop swiping left. You're home.

❝ Let us not take ourselves too seriously. ❞

Queen Elizabeth II, Christmas Day telly message, 1991.

Great British Public

The greatest thing about Britain is not the fact that we have the greatest roads, or the best schools, or the coolest politicians, or the fact that WHSmith *still* exists, it's that we have the loveliest, nicest citizens a country could ask for. After having given back most of the nations we once owned during our empire days, Brits today are the most-liked peoples on Earth, no doubt due to our XL bulldog spirit (now illegal) and our ability to "Keep Calm and Carry On", a mantra that has allowed us to keep calm when every other country is carrying on – in a better direction.

British public wrong about nearly everything, survey shows

According to the Independent, anyway.

. . . .

Brits call each other "Mate" not because they're friendly but because they don't want to ask you your name again and make everything awkward.

TEN (BRITISH) COMMANDMENTS

1. Thou shalt apologize, just in case
2. Thou shalt spend 45 minutes saying goodbye
3. Thou shalt always remember 1966

These guys are everywhere!

4. Remember thy supermarkets close at 4pm on Sundays
5. Thou shalt never forget the war
6. Thou will never take David Attenborough's name in vain
7. Honour thy barmaid and barman
8. Thou shalt not make a fuss (publicly)
9. Thou will wear no sunscreen on holiday
10. Honour no other Gods, except thy Gallaghers

Cashless Britain

Our first-class economy is so loaded with cash it has enough leg room to kick

*At one of the 11 bookies on your high street.

off as many foreign wars as we want. Hell, our hundreds of food banks are so stocked they don't need bailing out (yet), and every day there are more payday loan companies so desperate to just give us cash we're spoiled for choice! As our great British politicians declare, despite all evidence to the contrary, Britain's economy is doing just fine in a post-Brexit, post-COVID, post-Russia, post-Truss world. That said, if you've got a tenner we could borrow until next week that would be great. A pint ain't cheap these days.

. . . .

ICONS OF BRITAIN: MARTIN LEWIS
There's no one more bothered about saving us cash than "Money Saving Expert" Martin Lewis. It's all he bangs on about. Mate, eating Tesco's Meal Deals until next Friday when Nan said she'd give us a few quid is absolutely fine, chill out. Get a proper job.

. . . .

 **Fiver**

 **Tenner**

 **Twenty**

 **"Excuse me while I speak to my manager."**

It's legal tender, matey.

· ·

❝ Money, like manure, does no good until it is spread. **❞**

Ye olde British proverb.

· · · · · · · · · · · · · · · · · · · ·

Britain's artists are pro-poor! ↗

The Cost of Living

Despite frolicking in shimmering coastal waters surrounded by Astute Class nuclear attack submarines (and a bountiful supply of turds), things have become quite tough financially for British citizens lately. The cost of living – that's right, simply getting out bed – has become a crisis too burdensome to bear in Britain. Many of our 67 million residents struggle to afford the basic essentials, such as vapes, *Fortnite* bundles and Five Guys. Right now – and probably until the end of the next century – Brits around the country are desperately Googling "inflation" to try and understand what it means, because no one seems to have a clue – least of all the twits who keep inflating things.

Poundland – never disappoints!

≡ Lincolnshire Live

NEWS   SKEGNESS LIVE   IN YOUR AREA   SPORT   WHAT'S ON

NEWS

Man protests on pub roof after finding out price of a pint has risen

The customer was sent 'over the edge' when told his pint would be going up in price by 20p

LIFESTYLE   ≡

Man who realised it was cheaper to live in a 5* Turkey resort moves there

≡   ·   LancsLive

NEWS   IN YOUR AREA   CLARETS   ROVERS   PNE   SEASIDE

Cost of Freddo bar rises to almost 50p amid cost of living crisis

HOt TRANSSEXUAL
Busty Boobs English DD
£60 ECONOMY SPECIAL

TS-Lolly.com 24/7

"Economy special" – the price to beat!

Benefits of Brexit

Britain's great escape from Europe was a nasty affair, wasn't it? Brexit left the nation poorer, miserable, divided and more uncertain about the future. At least we think it did – it's hard to tell. We were all pretty poor, miserable, divided and uncertain about the future before Brexit. Now, however, Britain is well and truly on its own having "taken back control" from its evil overlords – the EU – even if four (five?) prime ministers lost their job in the process. If that's control, we'd hate to see Britain absolutely fucked. Thankfully, the nation is now more united than ever – against the Tories. For a nation that's survived two World Wars, both Ant *and* Dec and Trinny *and* Susannah, divorcing from the mainland has been easy-peasy by comparison. Besides, when you think about it, apart from peace, prosperity, stability, democracy, growth, free trade, jobs and the ability to live free and work in 27 countries, what has the EU ever done for us? We're better off without it.

❝ The great and the good will decide what is good for us and make sure that we get what is good for us, good and hard. ❞

Nigel Farage, *The Guardian*, March 2009.

when the going gets tough, the tough vote Leave!

A recent YouGov poll revealed just 31 per cent of Britons think Brexit was a good idea. What a mess! *Bregret*, anyone?

Party Politics

Britain is the birthplace of global politics. Our Parliament is a political powerhouse full of esteemed and elite big thinkers whose wisdom and leadership skills rise above their own self-interests, intellects and egos – and is where party manifestos are sacrosanct and no-one is above the rule of law. Ten Downing Street is also the most feared and respected political address in the world. It was also, as Boris Johnson demonstrated during his tenure, the best nightclub in London.

Britain is at its strongest when it unites behind a formidable prime minister, a statesman who devotes their entire life to king and country, leaders such as Tony Blair, David Cameron, Liz Truss and Rishi Sunak. We followed those great champions of freedom, truth and democracy anywhere...even when it was far, far away from freedom, truth and democracy.

. . . .

In 2022, 11 out of 12 bathrooms in the Houses of Parliament tested positive for trace amounts of cocaine, including a toilet close to then Prime Minister Boris Johnson's office. Party on!

. . . .

Just one in five Britons trust the
British Government.

No Context Brits
@NoContextBrits

LIVE WESTMINSTER

WHAT A
FUCKING
SHITSHOW

BBC NEWS BREAKING
UK Prime Minister under pressure
Labour urgent question on departure of previous Home Secretary
• Veteran Tory MP Charles Walker describes situation as a 'shambles'

Hear! Hear!

❝ Funnily enough, it was tractors I was looking at. ❞

Neil Parish, British politician (caught red-handed
watching porn in Parliament), *Sky News*, April 2022.

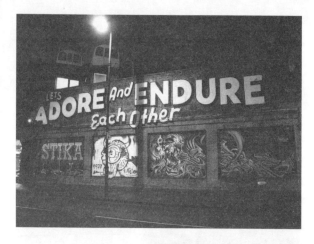

66 We use sarcasm as a shield and a weapon. We mercilessly take the piss out of people we like or dislike. And ourselves. **99**

Ricky Gervais, Time.com, November 2011.

My parents in their 30s

This would make a wonderful home to extend our family.

Me in my 30s

I'll never financially recover from this.

A financial fact worth spreading.

Brokeback Britain

Great Britain is great. We're not going back on that. And she'll always be great even when her pronouns become they/them. But if you stop and stare at the old girl for too long these days, you might just see a few cracks creeping in on her once flawless complexion. Dark bags under the eyes, crow's feet, saggy jowls, skin tags and sun damage. (Well, maybe not that.) Yep, today's Britain has a few unexpectedly baggy items in her bagging area. This metaphor, of course, alludes to Britain's high streets, healthcare system, government, national institutions and about 50 or so major British-based corporations, all of which are in desperate need of a facelift, and/or full-on frontal labotomy. Thankfully, Britain is not broken – yet – she's just "tired and emotional" and suffering an almighty hangover from a party that ended 30 years ago. So, today, as we demand more and more from our nation, let's all decide to give Britain a break and let the old girl enjoy a much-needed "duvet day" in bed eating Wotsits. She'll be fighting fit again in no time. We hope.

. . . .

66 The maxim of the British people is 'Business as usual'. 99

Winston Churchill, wartime speech, 9 November, 1914.

No Context Brits ✓
@NoContextBrits

GP surgery receptionists gearing up for 8am.

FUCK OFF

≡ News**hub.**

British cutlery company releases square-tipped knives that can't stab people

≡ BirminghamLive

NEWS   IN YOUR AREA   BLACK COUNTRY   VILLA   BIRMI

Man arrested for 'flashing penis' was actually showing Greggs sausage roll

What you doing today x

am in hospital xx

Today 12:51

Oh no why? X

Today 14:25

having my baby ah x

gutted i'm not out tonight man haha x

Britain's gone wild!

No Context Brits
@NoContextBrits

Of course Covid would say that.

BBC 👤 Home   Menu ▼   Q

NEWS   ≡ Menu

Business | Market Data | New Economy | New Te

Covid: 'People are tired of working from home'

🕓 5 hours ago | 🗨 Comments

British English

English has been the de facto language of Planet Earth for generations, famed for its magpie-like ability to "borrow" beautiful words from other languages and make them its own...before corrupting them into something horrific. Today, the graceful and poetic language half-invented by the world's greatest wordsmith, William Shakespeare, has been replaced by a new breed – a mongrel – of language that we now call British English. It's mostly swearing, if we're honest, with an array of inventive curse words, slang, puns, contractions and buzzwords that are nowhere near as big and clever as we think they are. Thankfully, even if no-one can understand us anymore, the English language still *sounds* fucking great, innit?

 No Context Brits   •••
@NoContextBrits

He was ahead of his time.

SHAKESPEARE QUOTE OF THE DAY

An SSL error has occurred and a secure connection to the server cannot be made.

 Shakespeare was the G.O.A.T. with words and shit.